Underneath
The Occipital Bone

Deborah Wood

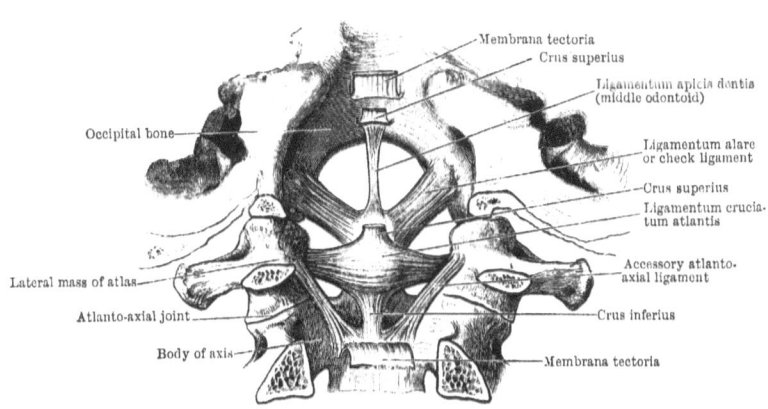

SPUYTEN DUYVIL

NEW YORK CITY

ISBN 978-1-959556-30-5

Library of Congress Control Number: 2023940191

For B & L,
I was always writing toward you.

CONTENTS

"Tu es celui qui écrit et qui est écrit."
—Edmond Jabès, *The Book of Questions*

THE DEEP FRONT LINE

The word anatomy means to cut things into pieces,
to forage for the truth,
so then, how to close the gap between ourselves and things?

Dear X,
I will not write letters anymore, not now, not in my sophomore year.
This will be my first letter after the last.

Like an alchemist, bringing beauty to the mundane,
there you were, climbing up the deep front line
from the sole of the foot to the tip of the tongue.

There I was, connecting myself to the ground,
pads of the feet and palms of the hands.

Dear X,
I paint brick walls white, trying to get back to that time.
I yell, "I am possibly lonely."
This is my difference.

This is me, in love with my subway line.

Like an alchemist, now you draw a circle
with the tip of your tongue.
And secondly, a dot inside of it.

Then, follow me down this passageway, that would be thirdly,
that would be clogged with language—making, imprisoning, molesting
with meaning, with your doing.

Dear X,
This is really happening
because the head unfolds the heart with the whole mouth.

No scissors, no tape, no glue, just folding
just the sea and air merging at dusk,
and then the guilt and anxiety because we cannot close the gap
between ourselves and things.

Dear X,
I am aware, but without structure.

You have to believe me
because, like origami, we are the present tense.

You have to believe me
because the bottoms of my feet are black with moving,
paper-thin membranes, wrapping.

Yet still, the degree to which the center can move down is severely limited
by the anchorage of the heart.

Paper-thin membranes, wrapping.

UNDERNEATH THE OCCIPITAL BONE

There are countless examples, such as there are twenty-four vertebrae for the twenty-four hours in a day. There is enthusiasm and he was on *Judge Judy*. There is Mrs. Dalloway buying the flowers herself. There are ventricles & channels and crimes of gaucherie. There are people dying in alphabetical order. And if you use ampersands I will sleep with you on the third date. There are tendons, ligaments, & bones, each more important than the next. Also, when they say symphony of flavors do they mean it? There are locations and things originate. There is cracked vinyl but still playing that song. There are conversations & conventions. Find a new form. There are three hundred-pound cows being butchered at the museum in the name of futurism and Isadora Duncan's scarf. There is me and I climb mountains & outdoor sculpture & lawn ornaments. This is that. There are countless examples of Parisian poems. There are swim coach drownings, and then interstitial fluid. Congestion. There are counted breaths. There is a balanced suspension in the spine. There are pictures of me crying. Sometimes things are multiplied by ten. Sometimes things are divided by twenty and rounded off. There are epicureans and bodies battered by wants. I am digital palpitation. I am diaphragm domed. I am ergonomically designed. There are cadaver labs. There is the hairpin curve of the birth canal. This is a tribute. You know who you are. There are alternating zones of hard and soft tissue. Here is the spinal column. We are a hidden pact.

AND THE ONE AFTER THAT

This is my intentional "to do" list. My inventory of moments. My body. Today and tomorrow. A text of dis-ease. I am ten fingers collecting things to burn. Call 9-1-1.

The possibility that we can be attentive. Colored pins on a map. Tracking. Harboring a fascination for the moment. Inventory life. Framing. Sewing. Diagramming life. Let's explore the hyphen between "A" and "B."

Write in green pen a daily attention, become meditation. Books of grammar. This is how I say "I love you." 365 different ways. This is how I say "I hate you" with just a pair of hands.

What if you are very boring? What if? What if? What if? Rhythmic possibility. Repetition will reveal detail, an attention, intention, invention, open field. Try this in red pen.

Syllables evolved from chewing. Coffee table books. Parking spots full and then emptied. Always key the one on the corner. The first and last lines of books. Underlining. The sleeping spaces of the homeless, my partner, my dog.

Why don't you step in front of my viewfinder? Where are you at noon each day? My secret diary of "to be" lists.

The present, this instant, and the one after that. You will need, you will need, you will need. Breath. Teacups with certain chips, the birthdays of drowning victims, perfectly measured cake recipes. The hidden error in the system. Time and time again. A concordance of Cyndi Lauper songs. The distance of time.

Open your eyes, wider please, take a look.

WE FORGET TO WRITE HOME ABOUT IT, OR ANYTHING, FOR MONTHS

I am swimming in the Arabian Sea where they spread the ashes of dead monks. I am wrapped in borrowed cloth, plain white, but threaded with gold. There are blue statues carved into the coastal walls, playing lifeguard to the apathetic. I swim farther. It is auspicious here and so I wear no nail polish. I am naked for the welcoming.

We are submarine bodies. Our cards are on the table. We are distracted by our new friends; they chant to find god. I chant because I am lonely for you. You draw on your forehead and your body becomes a temple of god. Our friends, they are looking for you.

Our submarine bodies belong to each other. I chant and build a place for you to tell your story with your hands. Your sternum lifts, your toes spread. Yes.

I search in between the stones for answers, for consciousness, and find the key. The key is to say "yes." So I whisper, yes, into your pancreas, your liver, your canyons, and in between each of your unbrushed teeth. I search for the concave in you. Sometimes I wish you were a girl. Sometimes I wish I could touch you like a girl.

Then it goes, my new friends, they chant to find god. I chant because I am lonely for you. One day my hair will be long and you will love me. I chant, yes, still.

We are on the tarmac, and we don't know where to go. You tell me a story with your hands, and in the middle of it we find home, a navigable space. In it, I build you a hut made of mud & sticks, and I bless it everyday at noon with fire & water.

We find home, and in it that space between form & potential. Then we turn our regrets into victories made out of "yes" & "no," unraveled secrets, pollen, and wet stone. We are a confluence of convex creatures. I am just waiting to be dismantled and then built again, my submergible body.

Tell me more, Mother Goose. Then it continues: we eat oatmeal everyday, I'd like to touch you more than twice a year, and there is no one I would rather eat oatmeal with, hands down. I prefer to eat it in your bed while you're at work, your key in my left pocket. I will put one hand on myself while keeping the other on your key. I am always trying to locate myself, but fail.

I am on Malaria Watch 2012. It is still winter. Sometimes watermelon juice, no ice, no sugar. Sometimes we play Ms. Pac-Man. Sometimes you love me, sometimes not. I am feverish, and I've lost track of time zones. I am lost in your canyons, and fatigued. I am bathing in this "yes."

SEVEN MORE WONDERS, AND THEN SOME

The most beautiful order of the world is still a random gathering of things insignificant in themselves. (Herakleitos, Fragment 40)

First there is that opening chess move, leading to a French Defense. There are good entrances and terrible entrances. Hesitating before that first kiss. Manipulating objects. Secrets. Phosphenes & tide pools. Palaver & comity. That said, we think of the dawn patrol, the added option of a foggy morning. Then there are commas and blizzards of brackets. Sesquipedalian musicians. Small objects, her laughter. Bullet points could help the collection of words on this page. Bullet points running down the bare walls, running, running until you can't breathe. Holding your breath. Let's not forget outgrown haircuts, layovers, record players, grammar workbooks, overzealous stirring, bonded atoms, and eyelashes saved in jars underneath propped-up windows. Saturday mornings—bookworms, cheese shop girls, and acute angles. A random turning. That poem on page 65. Your lack of a phone call. Your midnight good night text. Ignoring coincidence and calling it serendipity. A cat's paw in a cup of coffee. Turning to page 66. Proper fractions & synecdoche. Baby carriages & wheelchairs, propelling each other down the sidewalk. Sushi overload. *Invisible architecture.* The issues of this space. My grandmother's vernacular. The irascibility of spider bites hidden under jeans. His proud recalcitrance. Pungent foods, sweet, sour, bitter, and astringent instants, the space between typeface, descending stroke, a completing gesture.

THE TITLES OF MY PREMEDITATED INSTANTS

On the day I was born certain things were decided. I was to be incarcerated with grammar and confetti. I would write for lack of certainty. Continuity? I would crave the company of an upright piano. I will find a corner to put it in, then ignore it. My bedroom is crowded with 180-gram vinyl. I climb, explore, and exchange. I hear broken carousel music on Muscle Beach. Venice gives me agoraphobic asthma attacks. I think stop signs are red lights again. The lighting makes me look blown out, wind swept on the beach. I will find his technique so different, I think I am fucking a stranger every time. I fear the familiar. I study lachrymology. My imperfect present is a compulsion. I perform suburban middle class gestures. I commit dangerous acts of reading. "Come into my den," said the spider, et cetera. I will bowdlerize my daily life, but keep all of the objectionable passages. I ran out of ghosts, so I create more. A bibliophagist, I will devour you. I succumb to commodified mating gestures. I will masturbate to him for months before we meet. Now every Sunday I get naked and eat coleslaw, prefer deviled eggs. I will discover that the consequences of printing the wrong material are extreme, lose my driver's license in a toothless and angry strip club, eat sushi with a neck brace—adorned race car driver, see the key limes lose their color to the green bowl. My shoelaces won't stay tied. I am as random as August. I need a curator. I swallow certain letters for emphasis, subscribe to bankrupt philosophies, roll around the space of a pop song, always read the last line first. I keep certain characters such as the hyphen secret. I am a musical. Shhh. I make lists of the bands we can hate together. Repetition is beautiful, so I will fuck him tomorrow. I am another day.

THE CURIOSITY SHOPPE

There is a constant wind in my right ear. Please believe me. My plants are thirsty and listening. A desert-like wind in French Catalan, coughing, whispering to Eastern Provence. Please believe me.

Our predicate predates my subject: small, tangible objects. Please be mine. My object. Render me insensate: lacking sensation. Touch my object. Remember, here. There are wings pinned to bits of wallpaper behind glass, like arms with motion inside, waiting. There is a velvet painting overwhelmed by her blue-eyed stare, a borrowed twelve-string guitar. Listen to this. Listen to these objects. Closely.

Round the spine, finish the book—the "I" is always implied in printing. Objectified. My small objects, on top of a marble tabletop, half-eaten Japanese pub food, unused Vancouver travel guide, owls hanging on walls in threes: an extra, a couple plus one, what do we do? How do we decide?

The titles of our premeditated instants. My forty-two line autobiography, lazy dog, pencil sharpener hidden in plastic-covered globe. No space. No space. Hawaiian honey, honey, a rented room in West Hollywood, lazy cat, a shoebox blooming with tissues. Airspace.

Remember: everything is okay when refracted, another angle. Her plaintive stare, it could reform if I turned my head, turned away from, my broken mirror. Please believe me. A moveable type, agent of breakage. Listen.

We quest for the perfect context, the perfect text, a moveable type. Investigate the front porch, find an empty honeycomb, our collection of cardboard farm animals, watercress—look for traceability, when was it harvested? Our unsolved case.

Phantom noise, a constant wind, lapsed subscription, forty-two lines—a critical essay. Please listen.

Engineer this—slow down, study the tidal shifts, find the quiet between two things (there is a wind in my right ear), at the end of this line, next Monday afternoon at three, a resting place between two notes, G flat and A sharp, between two people unsure of where to next step, how to stop, stet? Left or right? Baseless. Recycled. The "I" is always implied. You must believe me.

AN AORTA WITH BRANCHES

Il n'y a pas de hors-texte. (Derrida)

Water removes the earth, changes the anatomy
of a tooth. We know this. So let's embrace the
rest of not knowing. Let's embrace intimacy with
things that are on fire.

Things are happening.

Truckee, California

His neck slopes, his shoulders hunched from too much reading. He leans into a car window, California tags. He says, the forty-eight minutes before sunrise are the most important of the day. He says, I am impossibly lonely. My eyes are the color of beets & chocolate. At nineteen weeks I was a large heirloom tomato.

I must have been looking down.

We speak of taking consciousness and turning it back against itself. We speak of how at seventeen weeks he was a turnip.

Things are happening.

Reno, Nevada

He inhales, *so,* exhales, *hum.* Let's explore the trajectory of bodies in orbit. So. Hum.

I like to be upside-down, on my hands. I have a really strong desire to reread all the Judy Blume novels. Or are they novellas? I want to tell you the story of my first kiss.

We were at a dinner party. We were discussing a town called *Homesick.* Then we see it while driving across the desert in a hand-painted gold Chevelle. Yes. We are in the middle of Nevada, in the middle of nowhere, and all of a sudden the car smells of onions.

And by the way, the emperor is not wearing any clothes. But the simple explanation is not always the one we want. So, hum.

Salt Lake City, Utah

He says, creating a map means ignoring everything in the world except one thing. A map of graffiti fills my dreams. Patterns of leaf light—

He says, this is what it means to live in a neighborhood. This is how it feels to be home.

I am in a corner. A cornea, watching.

We are in the middle of forty-five mile per hour wind gusts, our mouths full of iceberg lettuce, iced coffee in our guts, and rocks spelling, "I love you Mom," in the salt on the side of the road.

Whole and healed, while still imperfect, human.

Green River, Wyoming

He says, I see ghosts all day. I see girls in shoes that they can barely walk in. We are all dying. He says, you only love me in October. October is like hugging in sweaters. There is a coffee shop, a zebra painting hanging above your head, and it is October, so you love me and everything is okay.

I say, by the way, I will love you more when you learn how to play Smokey Robinson's "Being with You" on the ukulele.

We are all toppling over. So, hum.

Something is about to happen.

Lincoln, Nebraska

He says, we drove on the wrong side of the road. The salt flats and sulfites across the highway. If we drive across the country again, next time, we will drive around Nebraska. He says, if you were a state, I would visit you every day.

True stories are told without notes. I admit my desire to read all the Judy Blume novels. The summer I went to camp and I only ate candy, I need to tell you of this. The Mediocrity Principle, I need to explain this. I need to tell you, we don't have to move again. I want to tell you the story of my first kiss, one year after the summer of candy. I want to tell you of the Casimir Effect, the trajectory of bodies in orbit, my desire to throw pennies at Virgin Mary statues, to have a mouth full of universes and dirt.

We are talking about maps—the landscape of his background noise, the impulse to capture the whole world on a map. We talk of our welcome home party, even though home confuses me, and I believe that I may have misplaced it. We are doubters. We are commas.

Oh, and everything has a name. Supplements, everywhere. *Hum.*

Joliet, Illinois

He leans his head, full of hair, in the window, says, white is the color of yes. He says, the characters are all too human. I don't like any of them, until two days later I do. I love them all, in their imperfection, incompletion, and impermanence.

I love you all.

I just may be one continuous web of energy. I say, you help me to see what the weather is like.

We go to the same mall, and there is an absolute recognition of wanting. When we go sofa shopping, I think, is this going to be comfortable when I have the flu? We listen to what the breath says, and inside our dirt-filled mouths—whole universes and all of the galaxies.

You can live on plastic mangoes and milk alone.

Des Moines, Iowa

In Iowa he tells me I cry like the wilderness.

I am a flirter of prefixes. I am a prefix whore. I let him do things
to me with a mouth full of ante, contra, dia, extra, hypo, infra,
over, post, syn, trans, ultra, under. I am modified. A chemist of
words, I say, I accept.

I say, things are happening to me.

We are celebrants of the small batch, the sustainable, the hand-
tooled, and woodworked. We celebrate the upside-down, the
pickles, the whiskeys, & jams, white brick walls, tracking pigeons
in the park, our logographic systems, sweat glands and goose
bumps.

This path is not straight, it is diaphanous. This is a dialogue on the
mat, a plural practice.

Youngstown, Ohio

He says, we were discussing the new "no shoe" rule, and the fact that
I missed Cheyenne. The sides of the building say, "He cares for you,"
and you is me, and there are hitchhiking bedbugs in my suitcase.

I ask him to touch my difference. I say, owls are not what they seem.
So, hum.

We are discussing the difference between religion and culture, and
your barefoot driving, and your feet stink (but I like it just like I like
the smell of the sofa that the dog sleeps on), and my ABC store pen,
and Ben Kweller sounding like Weezer, and the dust bowl, and RUN!,
and Nebraska leaves something to be desired, and we should take up
smoking just for the road trip's sake, and the importance of mangoes
and milk.

We are listening to instructions on how to set up a buffet.

Things are happening. The heart is a muscle, and I work for you.
Doer.

Falls Creek, Pennsylvania

He says, just because something is inevitable doesn't mean it's bad.
He says, because an effect does not exist apart from its cause.

He has sweat glands and goose bumps; I glide my hands over both.
A twisted palette. A combination of cigarettes and French-pressed
coffee. There is ice melted on my tongue. There is the first pot of
coffee in a new apartment.

We know something is about to happen.

What to use as a navigational clue? A blue wall, the left or right,
connect four?

Goshen, New York

He says, the jawlines change in Brighton Beach. There is an Orangina store one block off of the boardwalk. He visits regularly. He plays the piano while facing the ocean swells. He takes passport photos two blocks behind the train. He will also travel to you. He considers it part of the mapmaking century. Every map, a world seen through a different lens. His own face through a different lens.

A living organism. A map shaving inches off of a pool of light.

To the royal sun lady in Brighton Beach—I say, it is November and you are a human machine, a hungry harvester of light. Your texture is foreign to me though ninety percent the same. You are a part of the mapmaking century.

We have no self-control. We yell at the cows, run! Run! They're going to eat you!

Our home, whole and healed, while still imperfect, human. So, hum.

Brooklyn, New York

There are four directions. There is balance. There is vertigo. There is a carpenter's level in my head. We may be allergic to life. We just may be. We resolve all our ideas on a grid—NY City's 1972 subway map, stacked plastic dinnerware, the Vignelli calendar, black and white letters spilling all over the front seat of the car.

We are very special birds that no one has seen. We are documenting hypotheticals. We are tearing up. Things are happening. Birders are so strange. So, hum.

So human.

NOTES FOR A GIRL

1.

It all started with my sewing class friend. It is noon again and today is the first day without rain and I am underlining everything.

2.

I am reading B's book. She is a hoax.

3.

Today I decided to be in a good mood because there are hearts quilted on the toilet paper and I made a sewing class friend.

4.

She's bespeckled.

5.

She othered herself with competitive swimming. Explored the limits of violence with the butterfly stroke.

6.

We stood on the steps of the Opera House and gave a traffic cop the finger. The bee mixed nectar with saliva, and saying "I love you" is so cliché. Meet me there, in the book, and glance, glance, glance each time you commit a descending stroke with your eyelid.

7.

In March, I always travel light. I defy gravity. Our seabed.

8.

Mostly I see green and orange.

9.

Unable to speak, she collects scraps. Figures the ways to construct a message—
realizes that names tell us how to do things.

10.

I dislike flight attendants. Being opposed to something is really easy.

11.

I love your hemisphere.

12.

Buy a zone 1 and 2 ticket from Pigalle Station, take the blue #2 line to Pere Lachaise not towards Port Dauphine but the other way. She hides there. She will be hiding there.

13.

She searches on Craigslist for an old Russian submarine to strip down to bare metal and use as a planter in my backyard.

14.

You could be anyone with the same name.

15.

I am being and becoming.

16.

There are wooden bowls of bananas and static radios and dirty sporks and thermostats with black tape over the numbers—we can feel what is right with our own bodies.

17.

She's a sandwich maker and amateur piano player. She has a page turner in her employ. The page turner has a tumor in his fingertip.

18.

One of the names of God in Hebrew is *place*.

19.

She stood there on her serif feet, eating a crepe, in between a taste and a reaction.

20.

A competing gesture.

21.

Those ladies taught me how to sew certain seams. My mother taught me the trauma of cutting my hair.

22.

This is my ground zero. This is my Edmond Jabès. This is breaking tablets and wearing black tights, and ignoring commandments. This is watching birdcage porn instead of doing homework. This is entering pass codes and drinking black coffee. It is French-pressed and not drip-dropped. It is writing itself on a red typewriter and I am surprised.

23.

Can you get cancer in your heart?

24.

It is my professor is a klepto. And more importantly, is it a nice scarf?

25.

Sandwich maker, that bench you sit on was made from cutaway diagrams, it was made in Northern France under the noon sun like grapes.

26.

I am officially stalking him now. He is my hero.

27.

It is striped cashmere. Keep it out of the light because the colors are fugitives.

28.

Let's revise the lunch poems and find something new. Perhaps a nap between pages? The way to form a perfect sentence in your sleep. A perfect stage for very boring dreams.

29.

Giving birth is a type of dismemberment.

30.

Noon: a way of holding infinite space.

31.

If this is all process rather than fact—
then, the grammar of transformation is my Bible.

32.

We played Monopoly across the table from each other, we held hands.
We went to see the buffalo in the park. We held hands. We went
to the pawn shop that only sells guitars, and made the man laugh.
You taught me how to construct my world with only a glance, a
descending stroke, a competing gesture. We held hands. The weight
of a curve. We went shoplifting together. We ran away, your hand in
my left, my shoes in my right.

33.

The bee mixes nectar with its saliva, and there are wooden bowls.

34.

This space, a nest of words, is distorted by her absence, the absence of
seasons, nesting.

35.

Forehead pressed to the wet ground, just above the blanket just missed, hands pressed together above the head in a position of prayer, Eleanor thinks of her "to do" list, his hands pressed to her back, a cervical biopsy round two, her lies, her truth, tumors and fingertips, her "to do" list. Forehead pressed to the wet ground, the basin of peace.

STALKING MARIE CURIE AT THE PARTHENON

Marie Curie reads my diary while I play the toy piano. Our song
sticks to my fingertips like tree sap, the theory of radioactivity. It
could be relativity, an activity of sorts. She walked before she crawled.
Relatively so. I sing and she reads, ashes spotting her forehead, the
pages of my diary splayed open.

In hot weather longer lines are ideal, longer limbs are prime, better for
the splaying out. Better for cooling off. It is August and she reads. I
figure, it's my diary, but she has two Nobels, so okay fine. I expect
some edits, but to no avail, Marie Curie only writes in the margin,
"grammar rules don't help you catch a train."

Marie, it is your turn now. It was my hour for like an hour. Marie,
Notre Dame made me consider conversion. Wide-eyed and famished.
I'm famished. Responding to sunrise. Fainting. Your mother and
sister, you gave prayer up. Looking up. Trading spaces. Places. The
Rue Dauphine, heavy rain, "Oh, Pierre." Social symmetry. Death
watch. The decision to conceal emotion, another reason.

RADIATE: Polonium and Poland. Ray. A mutual interest
in magnetism. To proceed in a direct line from or toward a center.
This is (not) here. From A to B. To send out rays, to shine brightly.
Donated your Nobel medals. For the cause. Your new country.
Uranium salts resembling X-rays. New elements. Wet forehead. The
creases in the palms of my hands, touching. Shine.

Marie, remedy your pockets full of test tubes. Your pockets containing secrets written in isotopes. Your desk drawers and the pretty blue-green light, secrets written in secret equations. Remedy. Your cookbook too dangerous to handle, hidden in a lead-lined box. A heart defect. My diary. A remedy. My syllables evolved from chewing, between consonants and vowels. A storm in a teacup, a blue-green storm in your pocket.

I am sitting next to Marie Curie. Paralleled, line to line. Windmills and kilowatts. Tasting. Dancing from the tip of my tongue to the roof of my mouth. Tasting, and Marie Curie dancing. An act of ceremony.

Do you still have pillow marks on your cheeks? Creases even your Nobel can't erase? Cutaway diagrams. Have you reconciled your face, distorted by your breath on the glass like Duras? Your lists of likes and dislikes? Rigorous artifacts, a book of your grammar, emphatic accumulation. My ground zero. A coded act of ceremony. Marie, get tickets for the dance and I'll take you. Marie, I love your hemisphere.

CURE: Remedy. From Latin. From Polish, to care. Madame cure me. Recovery of, release from a disease. Something that cures dis-ease. Ground it with a mortar and pestle. Marie the pretty blue-green light. Hypothesis. X-ray. The horizon view, permanent.

You rented a room, a primitive garret, for shelter. I stay across the street, across from the Sorbonne and look up into your windows, see reflections. Marie, my portrait sitter, turn your head left. I try hard to identify, reconcile and illuminate. Study the anatomy lesson. Marie, an asterisk still remains by your name. Let's review the history of touching. Diary pages. Utterance. An act of ceremony.

THE BOTANY OF GRATITUDE

All knowledge is a response to a question. (Gaston Bachelard)

Gaston, I loved you as a postman. My first universe, an envelope, torn paper edged in flecks of mornings, noons, and nights. Address the shelter of my imagination. Philosopher of my adjectives. Open that space to plead with the subjunctive. Open that space to find environment. To love with news and let me reverse. Please address my moment beside expired stamp.

Gaston, you will buy your own fish, choose your own cut of meat. You will create space for my poetry, space as my poetry. It is all white, we will love the white.

We need a new map to uncover the outside. Unveil the constructed. My doyen, uncloud my turbid eyes to green mistake, an inchoate touching mid-sentence. And if you be not able to bring a dream, then you shall bring for your trespass.

Wander the breaks of Montara. Sift through hours of meditations on the sand. Gaston, the sun bleached your dressage breaches. Yes, Solomon was a great master in botany. But you, the house, shelter of daydreamers. Only error, hidden tarpaulin.

Gaston, meet me at the Cliff House apocrypha filling your back pocket. Your tongue a clementine. Your voice dispensing vitamin. Your mind allowing for laughter. Your vernal body saying no, this fact is invention.

DEAR MR. JONSON,

The word palindrome should be a palindrome. This is very disappointing to me. Thanks, Mr. Jonson. Disappointment is contagious & plagues my bamboo plant. It began to green in Queens, then tried Brooklyn, upstate New York, drove across the U. S. of A. in a rented blue minivan unlimited mileage dubbed José. Listened to Berg's *Lulu*. Did a stint in the Mission, now patiently dies on Bernal Hill. I cut its leaves with orange handles. Nonetheless, I agree with you about Julius Caesar. I must get a handle on my sadness, my despair. Despair has the kiss of death. When sleep covers my eyes life becomes a palindrome and I am almost there. Almost there. There. My words are squared. Remember to breathe following the patterns of ellipsis. Always archiving & converting files. The unconverted carry a stigma. A rose is a rose is a rose, a red *A*, a red lettered day. I started the fire so I could dial nine-one-one. The unconverted carry a temptation older than Eden. Beside bamboo, a plant to derange my cat. Ben, you felt oppressed. All that trying. Molecules merely nourish, manifold & subtle. The unconverted marry underneath a sky. Crowded with the confusion of birds. The behavior of moths, consumed by fire. Forget how to walk. Join the ministry of the wasp & the orchid. Maintain a resonance. Speak a vocabulary of the unaccepted. Wishbones from thirty-year-old Thanksgivings. Four hundred years of replication. Removed because of sudden moves. Misgivings. Did you consider the promiscuity of death? The following sentence is false. The preceding sentence is true. Reuse because there is no such thing as recycle. Dig up and find the hidden benefits of disorder. I confess I saw my pride-upside down. I confess to witness the hidden benefits of disorder. Ben, your baroque metaphors turn me on. I confess while massaging the alphabet with my tongue, with my toes. I confess while tying cherry tails to make meaning. Index to middle. I fill my mouth before I swallow. Swallow without the ess. Wallow. Wallow will do.

COLOR THEORY

An equation is something for eternity. (Albert Einstein)

Solid, reliable brown is the color of earth and is abundant in nature. Light brown implies genuineness while dark brown is similar to wood or leather. Brown can also be sad and wistful. Men are more apt to say brown is one of their favorite colors.

Dear Marcel,

The batch of cupcakes I baked last night is almost extinct, but they left chocolate circles on my countertop. When no one is looking I lick them in lieu of a sponge. My tongue navigates the crowd of crumbs and vitamin bottles, each standing half empty in an attempt to avoid a cancer that is already there. Marcel, my cells are so very unfaithful. Did you know that there is a TV character for each of us, a doppelganger in Technicolor, admitting to us everything that we hate about ourselves? Hello?

My head hurts from amnesia. By the way, what are you doing Saturday afternoon?

Dear Marcel,

I have been having a problem of reference. A bad case of vertigo. I am searching for the point of diminishing return. Thou saucy fly bitten flirt gill!

Love,
Me

P.S. I think I've found it in Room 365, underneath your grey sweater, underneath the sleeping cat.

Black is the color of authority and power. It is popular in fashion because it makes people appear thinner. It is also stylish and timeless. Black also implies submission. Priests wear black to signify submission to God. Some fashion experts say a woman wearing black implies submission to men. Black outfits can also be overpowering, or make the wearer seem aloof or evil. Villains, such as Dracula, often wear black.

Dear Marcel,

Since you left, relegating me a bride bare missing her bachelor, I've had a collection of fits and now choose to have breakfast with the shades drawn, lights off. I painted the bare bulb black with the Sharpie pen you left on my night table. I painted my nails black and streaked the walls. Every morning I wake up and re-ink black hearts on the palms of my hand to replace the ones that have hearted the sheets, the creases in my face. The white cat, also now black, bleeds onto the naptime sheets. Since you left I only eat plums, cherries, Cajun fish, black beans shadowing rice, chew my nails, paint chips from the basement, strands of hair, and dark dark chocolate. When you left, that very night actually, I had a dream where my eyelashes were burnt orange underneath, my lids could not stay shut in a Ziploc madness, and then my eyelashes fell off and grew into black tea leaves, black dahlias, and DNA.

A small package should be arriving for you soon.

Warning—

Dear Marcel,

I've been searching the pages of my texts—left margin, horizon, right margin, waves of ink falling onto the beach, spreading letters, meaning onto the page, into the world. But, I can't find your letters. Not one. I searched the compartments of my ancient advent calendar, found brackish opinion, landed on the bank of beware. But, not one.

I miss the perfect absorber of light, the best emitter when heated, you.

To pass the time I study the color shift in stars, try to find an opening. The violent birth. I find our beginnings between the channels on the radio, leave the leftovers un-refrigerated, play the black sheep of my family, propagate the propaganda, eat carbon chips, fetishize priests and judges, the leftwing bloc. While listening to The Damned, the sunlight stinging my eyes I question myself: how to better love an insufficient?

The most emotionally intense color, red stimulates a faster heartbeat and breathing. It is also the color of love. Red clothing is noticed and makes the wearer appear heavier. Since it is an extreme color, red clothing might not help people in negotiations or confrontations. Red cars are popular targets for thieves. In decorating, red is usually used as an accent. Decorators say that red furniture should be perfect since it will attract attention.

Dear Marcel,
Tomorrow I will practice the two kinds of giving up, realize looking is for down, the sun for setting.

Currently the most popular decorating color, green symbolizes nature. It is the easiest color on the eye and can improve vision. It is a calming, refreshing color. People waiting to appear on TV sit in "green rooms" to relax. Hospitals often use green because it relaxes patients. Brides in the Middle Ages wore green to symbolize fertility. Dark green is masculine, conservative, and implies wealth. However, seamstresses often refuse to use green thread on the eve of a fashion show for fear it will bring bad luck.

Dear Marcel,

I wanted to let you know that Allan died last night after sustaining injuries, after attracting the gangrene, after having bitten his tongue after stumbling on the sidewalk in front of my house. Isn't it strange what a stumble can commit? He was distracted by the hue of my key lime—filled mouth, said it appeared to him as a mirror, a finger pointing at the moon. (By the way, I don't think my transgression is important here.) We really are victims of our own mass—we all have days when we trip up the stairs. Anyway, I told him to see the school nurse for his heraldic aspirations and the submerged bullet fragments from the trip you both took to Watervliet. "Unmovable and inter-digital," he said. Anyway, his skin became green and rose like the sun, mimicking the future. He demanded that I find other uses for leaving chalk blueberries from love impact and I thought of you. Then I asked him to do it again, but louder. With a halting stagger he said, "That's friction fit," and, "I heart you." Striations. Now that he is gone, I realize that there are factors, ingredients such as sunlight, our signatures, and soot that all comprise his epilogue. Your prologue.

By the way, I sent you a watch. Check it every hour. Please do not bite your tongue, Marcel. Can you hear the sound of me spinning? I am behind the roman curtains, three flights up, and I will fold into you. The gesture, a contagion, your epilogue.

Oh Marcel, I loved his scraped kneecaps.

Dear Marcel,

Please call Stella. Ask her to bring these things with her from the store: six spoons of fresh snow peas, five thick slabs of blue cheese, and maybe a snack for her brother Bob. We also need a small plastic snake and a big toy frog for the kids. She can scoop these things into three red bags, and I will go meet her Wednesday at the train station. When you speak to her please implement vowel shortening and non-aspiration so that she can understand you.

Marcel, what would you do if you knew that you could not fail? I think that I would study the sex lives of octopuses. You know, their entanglements resemble soap operas. My doppelgänger stars in one. They act out their petty rivalries sometimes even while keeping their mating arm inserted fully. Sound familiar? Do you understand what this means? The courtship rituals of octopuses—like sudden oak death, we must find the roots.

P.S. My friend's cat died, but she is eight months pregnant with a son, so I feel like that makes it even. Anyway, that kitty litter can be evil to the pregger ones. Now, she is going to name the boy after the cat— before the cat died, she was going to name him after Miles Davis. The cat won.

Cheerful sunny yellow is an attention getter. While it is considered an optimistic color, people lose their tempers more often in yellow rooms, and babies will cry more. It is the most difficult color for the eye to take in, so it can be overpowering if overused. Yellow enhances concentration, hence its use for legal pads. It also speeds metabolism.

Dear Marcel,

I wanted to let you know that I have moved to a peculiar Californian town that built an underground tunnel to save toads from the potentials of vehicular frog slaughter. Don't worry though: I still love mayonnaise, butter, and Jewish men. Barry, Jerry, and Larry come to mind. Gluttony is still my sin of choice. My world is wonderful. I read in the news today that you can use a lemon to sanitize a chopping block. Thought you might like to know. A lemon can also whiten fingernails (though yours are usually bitten off), decorate on the cheap, and fade tea stains from cloth. There was something about the probabilities in the game of Monopoly, that Iraqi children are worth less than American children, that over-packing tops the biggest travel mistakes.

Marcel, I'm writing because my next-door neighbor's home was invaded and I'm scared. Simon is thirty-eight; he lives next door to me. Last week, on September 9, he said that he was sitting home alone masturbating and watching a porno when a small masked man holding a gun came down into the basement, and started to videotape him. This is what he told the local paper. Before the intruder left, he fed Simon's dog some mushrooms and the dog died. His dog's name was Max. Simon got a new dog yesterday, another chocolate Lab, and named him Max. He is an eighth, like Henry.

Marcel, I'm scared that he knows it was me.

The color of royalty, purple connotes luxury, wealth, and sophistication. It is also feminine and romantic. However, because it is rare in nature, purple can appear artificial.

Dear Marcel,

I made a beginning and then I left it. I ran away, could not stop looking back.

There was a dog barking at the moon hanging over the fireplace, surrounded by six hovering Cuban Emeralds of the avian persuasion— three males and three females, but only two pairs. Two remained solitary. Perhaps not by choice, but by biochemical fate. Yet still, each and every male defended its territory with song and flashes of iridescence. Marcel, do you ever crave the symmetry of dying on the same day you were born, like Shakespeare?

This morning I woke up supine after dreaming of monks wrapped in orange and maroon robes lining the halls of a cafeteria. It was there in that subterranean layer of waking life that I felt like a tourist who could not find her way home. I felt a fatuous prescience when I woke up, and I decided to find which museum walls hid that bride stripped of her bachelor. My doppelgänger. I traveled south.

Brides wear white to symbolize innocence and purity. White reflects light and is considered a summer color. White is popular in decorating and in fashion because it is light, neutral, and goes with everything. However, white shows dirt and is therefore more difficult to keep clean than other colors. Doctors and nurses wear white to imply sterility.

Dear Marcel,

Remember when we traveled south in a spontaneous moment of boredom? We had decided to look for M, our general manager. MapQuested Calle Fuego. Drove to Mexico City, the Pedregal section, and camped out under a lemon tree in a grove of avocados. We camped out until each piece ripened and fell off their respective limbs. Disengaged. It took some time, but we filled the empty space with badinage and sensed the compression within each moment. "I've got the dismals," you said before creating an absence where you stood. I went to grab two cups of coffee, one for me and one for you solitary in our vigil. I paid in pesos. Walking out of the café the man in front of me held the door in an everyday act of politeness. I thanked him, but only now realize that it was M. He disappeared behind the city of cardboard and tin roofs, disengaged. You had decided to become a gyrovague and left. Life had been discommoding. Standing there alone under the naked trees I thought of my friend, the one who faked the crucifixion on Christmas Eve with two girls he had just met. It was not contrived or planned. It just occurred, like this. Tears down his face. Tears down his back. Deconstructed flesh in pixilated monochrome, red. A flute of columns in pure view. After the 25th he was changed. He collected veined leaves, concealed them in the plastic wrappers of microwave dinners. He ate banana peels. He shot down the honeybees that stung behind the aluminum shed.

Marcel, in that lemon grove, crushed by the instant, I created lists of hope. I always keep one in secret. Marcel, sometimes I hope that you will move near the ocean in time for the eustasy.

Marcel, please leave these things precisely as they are, untouched.

Dear Marcel,

As of late, I have been concentrating on the preservation of coffee
and the cult of the embrace. I string festoon aqua faux pearls to wrap
my ankles, pretend you are here, wrap the napping cat. I want to be
part of a gang. I want to carry the title of head tea granny, gravitate
to where cupcakes are sold. I haven't left the house in days, but don't
worry I always wear sunblock just in case.

Dear Marcel,

The Cuban Emerald hid my secrets, stored them in his wings,
simultaneous layers in blue, yellow, green, secrets blending upon each
and the other—creating a mirage of truth.

The color of the sky and the ocean, blue is one of the most popular colors. It causes the opposite reaction as red. Peaceful, tranquil blue causes the body to produce calming chemicals, so it is often used in bedrooms. Blue can also be cold and depressing. Fashion consultants recommend wearing blue to job interviews because it symbolizes loyalty. People are more productive in blue rooms. Studies show weightlifters are able to handle heavier weights in blue gyms.

Dear Marcel,

There has been so much talk. Schadenfreude interrupting the momentum of your silence, so that I feel myself de trop. Reading essays on friendship without one in sight. I continue with my ceremonies of intensity, rituals of sensation. It is all very similar. I take my 3 a.m. pill with the windows open, glance across the architecture, use my index finger to carve unpredictable angles in the dust, write my own narrative with the mind. All that waiting. I take naps in a Soft Scrubbed tub, while seagulls map undiscovered archipelagos above my head in the glass. Consider open-heart surgery. Would it help me navigate the ambiguous folds in time? Remember that book? Blanched. Marcel, don't you worry about me, Bakelite jewels still adorn my painted fingers and I eat *tortas* while mouthing the words for the ingredients in French, imagining the semblance of my missing lover. Missing you. Nightly, in a box by the unmade bed, I file away my collection of paint samples from Arcade White to Relentless Olive, and then read stained pages to discover what occurs in the hills at night. While you inhabit the three-lined text, I obsess over the uncertainty of the next.

My today is just like tomorrow, yesterday, but wholly unlike your today, any day. Is my blue your blue? Is your Quixotic Plum mine? Every day seems like a Friday or Monday, but I am patient for Wednesday, a Halcyon Green.

Dear Marcel,

I am still searching for your letters. I am sure of being extinguished, always read the last page first, first the last line, the goodbye, and then again, repeat, renew, revise. Marcel, please, please repeat the first one last.

Marcel, thank you.

THE MORNING AFTER SUMMER CAMP

It is well known that you are a great collector of all sorts of people. You've built a human menagerie, and I want to smash it. Yes, your collection of glass, in bits & pieces—the prettiest of celadon, on the floor. Mermaids drowning in a shallow sea.

It is well known that my guru speaks of grace, but I still can't find that page in my dictionary. I look, then quit. I reach my arms to the sky, legs split in hanumanasana, and settle in. I search my own monkey mind, and try to forget yours.

I have been living close to the ground, letting go of everything that doesn't serve me. "Goodbye," I say, my bones sinking into the ground. But, my bones sink alone, and the park is screaming out for our company, my words are lonely for our camping.

You are a catholicon to my mermaid, my phantom feet, a permanence found. You could be anyone with the same name.

Our moral turpitude, daily. Our Sundays, crowded with fuschia pink fingernails, twenty-dollar brunch eggs, a flirtation with harissa, & kissing before noon. We are snakeskin heels & heirloom tomatoes, crowded teeth. We are the fog that requires the wearing of tights.

But, the "our" is always changing. The "we" is always running away, then back, then in circles. We are a book of fragments. We are dearest syncope.

Yes, my heart San Francisco, you are my scalloped edges.

The morning after, remind me of this assignation. Remind me of how you collapse into your joints, surrounded by glass. You are my dirty laundry, folded and placed on the bed.

You are the prettiest of celadon, scattered on the floor. You are all of the mermaids drowned, a scattering of ashes.

A HISTORY OF READINGS

To feel the combination of words on your tongue. Letters mimicking flavor. Form. Tactile. Pressing fibers. Pressing fingertips. To touch. I misheard. Looming ahead, the horizon. Margins. Cover me. Bond me. In that way. A series of knots along pieces of string for accounting. To care for. Cover me. To touch. Warp the weft. Measure my sentence in deniers. One is thinner than the other. Rub me with acetate to increase my shininess. Velvets & taffetas. Embroider the fibers to extend lashes, to be seen. Witness. Expose the fine lines to sunlight. Morph my morphemes, then grammar. Stray from my tongue. Slick and impervious to water. The alginate is dissolved, leave the open area.

LETTER TO AN UNDERTAKER

The pasta is al dente. There is an inherent paradox in this. Forget
that and discard the fibers, because it's Thursday morning again.
Why don't you whisk together the minutes you can no longer tell
apart. The safety coffin, you can ring the bell to signal breath. Whisk
together the small reddish-brown seeds of grains of paradise. Cells
continue to divide unfaithfully hidden by expensive astringents and
lotions and makeup and skin. A candle will be held to the mouth.
Resuscitation will be attempted by stimulating various parts of
the body with juices of onions, garlic, and horseradish, whips and
nettles. Excessive noise. Neighbors. Toast two tablespoons white
while handling objects that haven't been touched for so long. Dust to
dust. Simulation. Objects—yours and mine. Ours. The invention
of the stethoscope in 1819 removed the need from these extreme
measures. Ashes, ashes, we all fall down. This is my message in a
bottle. Unable to see through the myth of status, possessions, and
unlimited consumption. You should walk the dog. No time, no time,
no time. Greedy for the past. There are no reflex functions associated
with coughing, gagging, eye movement, blinking, or dilation with the
pupils. Greedy for the past. You should pretend to forget to return
that phone call. But, the cells of the body could be kept alive. You
should add the fabric softener. During the previous test the carbon
dioxide level of the blood has risen above the point at which breathing
is normally stimulated. Proof. The spotted gum rubbing against
your naked feet, its oils poisonous for protection. Cats in the wild.
Rubbing against the wood. You will rub against me. But sutured by
time. Intervals. Inserting dyes. The recycling of materials. And if
you are a connoisseur of you, then me, well then write and follow this
prescription. Permanent & irreversible. Loss of cognitive function.
Death of the cerebral cortex. The ice harvest in my freezer. The
doorbell is so scary, ringing. A flat electroencephalogram, indicating
an absence of brain activity is often used for verification. The

unknown on the other side of that ridged glass, smoked, invading your suburban home. Your guilt immediately shows and your cells continue to grow and divide unfaithfully. Your citadel on fire. Flat-line. Burnt to the ground. Dust to dust. Your dust, ashes. Some comatose patients can recover. You will expect this diving response. Diving response as porn shot. The tongue populous, a pomegranate, errant and bursting. Your angle is great. An asymmetry between life and death. Evidence of irreversibility. With only trash day as your way of counting, of keeping time. You scoop the kitty litter sandbox, collect the week's compostables. Finally. Cut down each box with the box cutter, then what? Thursday morning. Greedy for the past. While mimicking the future. The present consumed by lies. Lies in waiting. My ladies. We all fall down. A dervish. The whirling operatic and addictive. Blue, bluer, bluish, blue. The veins puddling the skin, surfacing. Each revolution an adaptation. Ashes. Your love for perfectly cheap chardonnay paired with Thai food. Your song. A patience of language. Archipelagoes of words on the tongue. Lactic acid. The margins of your cheeks. Ransacked. No time, no time, no time. The body temperature will increase again due to the metabolic activity of the bacteria and other decomposing organisms. Permanent cessation of electrical activity indicates the end of consciousness— you will see. A complex reaction.

PLEASE REMEMBER

The table of contents, a lonely poem separated by an empty page.
Comrades. The table of contents, a poem. Displaced. A body
without its body. A breeze recalling a vertigo. I move around the
house through piles of papers, in all seriousness, a demeanor in
commiseration, asphyxiation, my fish blowing bubbles with straws
in the pond, keeping time. My steps are feet filing under the "to do"
sign. A geometry of cells dividing and then multiplying unfaithfully
under the skin. A geometry scaling the tips of the breeze.

Another and again. Lather, rinse, and repeat. That was fun. I rub
your sleeve with the tips of my fingers. Ask, how do I write your body
without difference? Parallel words. My book rubbing against your
book. What interests me here is the repetition, what interests me here
are the dervishes. Their covered thighs, powdered lids hiding their
pupils, but looking toward the sky. Chroniclers, mapping the circles
underneath our feet. The ritual of washing and shaving a head, a dog-
eared page,

a wish.   Mine a campaign of words.

HOW TO BE REMEMBERED WHEN YOU ARE NOT, NOT, NOT

Consider the causes of inflammation. Fabric stuffed to our benefit in shapes of lizards, hippos, and ducks. I can make the choice to believe him. For our benefit. Consider inventing daytime—lights & leafy vegetables, lettuce & kale, some tape. Bedizened. Smuggle yourself back to that time, and let the moment school you. Protect yourself. Don't forget to bring the summer wine. Ask: Do you have a room with a better view? Ask: How does it feel to be a secret? Suddenly here, suddenly gone. But persist as an abbreviation, in the middle of hunting season an amative forty-point buck. A screened-in porch. We haven't located us yet. Give refuge. Ensure the seams are sealed because there are laws to protect us from each other. Economy, sweet lime, my convent. Remember the swollen irises, all participating in a common cabal—encapsulated possibility. Remember water is very heavy.

Thank you, I will watch time lapse.

DID YOU KNOW THAT THERE ARE LAWS TO PROTECT US FROM EACH OTHER?

Trust me. An improvement since the beginning of time. Once upon a voidness. The first wave. Before and after the ocean became a mirror. New Wave hair. Triple-non-fat-half-soy macchiato. Thank your god. The winds began to breathe; cream churned into butter. Antibiotics. The people knew that in order to survive they would have to become organized. We mimic the sun in shape. Calisthenics for my shape. My story is completely true. Without cause, without end. I am a fraud, greedy for the past.

[Each person has their own plant. Each plant produces a corn fruit. Each day the fruit is eaten. Another world appears.]

The winds began to breathe. Many people made him king. He brushed my hair with a spoon. My story, hundreds of little bits. A photograph of another. Greek statuary, bigger at the top. Now fighting and stealing, shopping and viewing. Lost fruit. Macrobiotic. Either you agree with me or you are a fool. The most indeterminate places. Enacting the impossible exchange, from bleached roots. Found at the mall. The beginning always ends,
he points at the news, says it's a rerun.

VINYASA

Leaves of paper make the pages. Each individual filament, my
middle name. Progress. You make the exterior cover. Intertwined
fiber: paper and mustard greens, language and epilogues, rainbow
chard, Meyer lemons, my maven, us: speaking across time. Creating
an atlas of tastings. A dedication. I'll undress you, my almanac,
in purple argyle and everything. That woven need of folding, then
unfolded.

Two tender ribbons of udon, flexible. We are undercover. Cross
section. Glued. A lama of the profession for the cutting of paper and
steel. The timbers. Leaves of plastic you isolate. Old bedsheets or
pillowcases are perfect. A needle and I pass the spinner, finger heavy.
I am the nails and the holes. I will not die wholly, but soon. This
stops transmission. Plastic lock of closure. Lightning. Triage. Our
bodies move in a calligraphy. A mandala crossing the lines. Sieve
like screen, rapid-fire knowledge, intertwined fiber, our pages—

HERAKLEITOS, WHAT DO YOU THINK?

The Danube could be a river, a world, a word, a place, or a crossing
of the English Channel or an island on the Serbian side with the tent
up or a route through the canals of France barring the lock and the
stolen trailers. We did not know what to do. The Danube could be
the sound of a thief stealing the morning and dragging it thru villages
by two bicycle wheels by building a new trailer in the hotel parking
lot. The Danube could embrace me. The Danube could embrace
human power or be a bike path (of sorts), a communication, a puzzle,
a question to a question, a dolly, a reservoir, a dam, a damn. What
is the difference between the water below and the reservoir? The
Danube could bring us to the Black Sea with the assistance of the
current, a currant in the mouth of a human, a river, a current pushing
my eyes toward Croatia. The Danube could be a song, a swan, or a
moment to listen, to hear, and to compare the weight of silences. The
Danube could be memory, the chase, the opportunity to step twice in
the same—

DEAR,

What is infinite to you may just be a sentence to me. Do what is
timely.
Like the owls hanging on my wall in threes. Draw them in fours
so that no one is ever lonely. I believe in you.

Remember the Golden Nugget in Baldwin Place? Remember
Amanda Rosenberg from Louis Drive? Can I research fire?
That word is mine.

You are your own architect. You have a fever upstairs.
Commit acts of attention indiscriminately. Love me indiscriminately,
and then love some more.

Because the moon always looks good, especially under a monsoon
sky—
look it up.

Change a comma in your daily life. Turn the page.
Divide complex fractions while drinking Turkish coffee.

Because the moon always looks good under a monsoon sky—
look it up.

INVITATION TO A DINNER DATE

We are the field guide to fossils. We are walking in the valley of the
page, like Hansel and Gretel, breaded & braided, let's try. Let's try and
get lost. We are seated at table nine. In between the theory of relativity
and that boy with trapezius wings. We ordered a Sylvia Plath moment
because I have too much tea in me, and you too little. We have a family
missing cousins and aunts, but neighbors abundant, we are becoming the
disreputable guests on the block.

We are an instant message. A personal hello. I approve.

Next door, the evening patrol. We are two sneezes and a closet door
closing. We are salt when placed on the tongue, asthmatic and contracting.
I promise. We are all confined to the coastal margins, we are all dependent
on the electorate, whether glazed with rain or not. Red or blue?

How well equipped are you?

Let's stick out our tongues and hope to catch some meteoric debris. Let's
play out the script, above the equator, talk about spaceships, swim in the
opposite summer. We are just two heating elements. We are capable of
manipulating objects. Let's try. The sycamore gives shade and sheds its
bark, it sheds shade and gives bark. We are the browsers & grazers in aisle
five. Sifting through brown rice and semolina, we are still seated at table
nine.

We are exploring those secret knots. We are exploring a series of
disorienting urban spaces, a coterie, a category,

lettuce crowding the plate, gems crowding the lettuce in a standing
ovation.

We are an instant message, a personal hello, I approve.

WHILE YOU SHOP THE MARKET IN HONDURAS, HERE MY OPEN AIR

Pardon my reach as I putsch across the table, the cake shop, reaching for your face of historical rivers, brio water. Say grace over sprouted bread, "the Lord is a shoving leopard," Thanatos and the anthology of my acquaintance. Reading Japanese design text over pink & green lawnchairs, percussionist prayer, beside hipster bike brigade, gang of hoodies. Listening to Gang of Four. How do they get them to stay on their heads? How feeding gives pleasure in cotton against unshaven legs. Remember to breathe and then hold it again for pleasure. Beneath the canopy of branches in late October. Pardon my reach. It's too electric. The font is too "Dead Can Dance" and library card. Borrower's name & date please. Metonymically speaking. I am in a vowel mood or note, say please ma'am. It's too electric monkey. Give me a resonance laced with orange peels. Give me the baby elephant walk, clipped. Stone table & Midwestern dialect. Give me metal on my finger for lack of language. Return & explain.

HOW TO KISS

My accumulation of Air Supply songs. You found. A quirky diction every day. A biopsy. A common gulag body of ordinary dancing. Undulate yourself free. A body diagramming and tracking, but always doubting. Guided by a pocket compass. Oh look, Saturn. Proximity, a moving association. Dewey decimated. Brought randomly but criminally. Sugar and glowing rings. A cat named Yoko Ono. An indication of kin and comparison. I am relative to you. A blink and you will disappear, I blink. I disappear giving rise to new fonts and simple characters. Secret characters. Irregular print. A biopsy, my fossil-skin—a root, a cutting. Let's calibrate. You will bring a world of things but stop short—I will aim for a third song, a song found in disjunction. Get yours. The archeological site of your gesture. Fill this lacuna with my days. Fifth song. Fill this with calumny, with amity. And all of those cowboys watching, leaning in. For sugar.

LET ME SHOW YOU MY SNOW GLOBE COLLECTION

Only humans complicate our lives—there are many paths to the truth, start walking. (Sri Swami Satchidananda)

If letters are diagrams pointing to the source, then explain the parts, operation, engine. If letters are marked by lines of language, strings, pearled, words forming chains of meaning, sentences. If letters are marked by lines from "Dear" to "Sincerely." Proof of existence.

Dear Louis K.,

It is hard to escape the permanence of address. A pencil may not do it, nor erase. Extinct like minerals, home, gem, ash. Just say no. There are small hills of mud under the trees, and you can use these to build the structures in your mind. Spooning to shape earth and water. Spooning to shape skin against skin. Skip the page. Miss that train. It is overrated and full of error. Or add three tablespoons of sesame oil and apply the paste on the full body of the patient. Help to erase their mother tongue terror. Find geometry, find Pennsylvania, find home. Or not.

If letters—Diagram of the heart. Of a cell. Your anatomy. Tattooed body. Diagramming story. Fathom map. A chart mapping the way home. To delve into and unearth meaning. Network. Nice to meet you.

Dear X,

Witness. Your arm reaching for mine to make meaning. The room is small. The book of hours, and then some days. You told me that I reveal different things about myself when viewed from different distances. You told me no design system is perfect. You told me there was a letter, but some letters get lost, some people become letters at the end of the alphabet, not all letters arrive on time. I point out the absent commas. I wrap the day in butcher paper and send it FedEx. Signature required. Your question is the answer, you are laughter, a security breach. You told me to exhale and recycle the universe. You told me to catch the wind. You told me you are usually successful. You are successful. Dear, you used the six broken ribs excuse for way too long. Place your feet on the ground, acknowledge the many paths, start walking. The body insists, a person can only teach what he actually believes to be true. You are successful. The body insists, revolving. Revolving, we are not free.

Dearest Lyric who documents with diagrams, defines on the page without shame, the breath in the body, from sacrum to tongue, diagrams which document process. From birth to death. I walked before I crawled. The seven geological layers, lower mantle, and oceanic crust, stratify me. Dissection.

Dear D.,

You stood on your head, hands free, and smiled at me upside down.
An articulation of the body. I mimicked you, explored how my edge
behaved. My ribcage filled with perspective and timed gestures. You
taught me the grammar of transformation. You taught me a competing
gesture, complete. My kidneys ached with thirst and my ego even
more. I was surrounded by people collapsing into different bodies. I
wanted to wrap myself in tinfoil, cut out two holes for my eyes, and
close my body, shut safe with sparkly heart stickers.

Diagrams pointing—How do you work? Origami. Tree outside my
second-floor window. Electric current. Draw a Venn diagram to show
my function in the world, this country, this city, this building, this
block, this room, this desk. Write me.

Dear Dharma,

This is real life. These are the pitfalls of nostalgia. I kept drawing
the box I came in, and you kept burning down my house. You are a
lover of analogies, you are a lover of gesture, that gesture of sewing
through wood with words, breath, and poses. We played the game of
observer and observed, you and I revolving, revolving like dervishes
until we thought that we were free.

Dearest Documentary, if *we are a landscape of all we have seen,* then
my poem is a limb of the diagram of life. Of witness. Your arm
reaching for mine to make meaning. A contemplative engagement
with something other than yourself.

Dear Lou,

Earlier gurus used to eat their medicines before prescribing them.
Their mouths were filled with gem ash. Dear Lou, there is that dis-ease
of accumulation, excess of impressions, of over-consumption, of home.
Use pen not pencil, then leave unfinished. Start a revolution. Leave
plans and more questions. Oh, home. Leave the absence of the proper
order, skin for that curve of the spoon, ash.

If letters are constellation, then explain the parts, operation,
engine. Paint by process. *You are the one who writes and is written.*
A wandering. Force yourself to get lost, then find your way home.
Dissect my sentences, word by word, from noun to verb. My
grammar lacking. Archeology for proof of existence. Constellations,
instructions, manuals. Let's communicate.

Dear Me,

There is too much counting, the body insists, and I see.

Today is the first day without rain and I am underlining everything.
That which is marked by lines. "A" to "B." Intersecting then leading.
Left wanting. Satisfied. Wanting more. Accompany and illustrate.
Paint by numbers. Stay in the lines.

Dear X,

Our bodies are a walking narrative, interrupted and fed daily. Starving and left wanting. Line by line, starving for paragraphs made from bones, tangents of muscle and story. Dear X., please interrupt me. Please feed me, I'm walking. Let's build worlds to play in tomorrow. Let's liberate the dervishes from their revolutions.
Write this. Paint by spine. Vertebrae. Delineate. The lines on your palm creating an awning of meaning. The typical syllable, a rhythmic alternation between consonants and vowels. Evolved from chewing. What does it look like? Diagramming fact married to hidden error. Accidental beauty. What do you look like?

Sincerely, I am yours.

FOR SOME IT'S HUNTING, FOR SOME, ANCHORAGE

Your skin an umami alongside but on my tongue. Milton forgot to read
that last and final line. Scratch that tale. You went to the museum
just to look at a corner of the Rothko. Came home three hours late.
Cogitate and *jai*. Full of earth your mouth opens to mine. I take
all I can hold, then want more. You just know it is all going to be
downhill from here. Verbal chess. Full of earth. Why do people wear
shirts of Ché, but not Fidel? The family radiation kit, a chemistry set
of myth, now. Next to your plastic Davy Crockett pencil case and
Queen of Hearts costume. What. I touch myself with your Queen on.
Dimensions. Your protester doll, vinyl with fake fur hair. *I'm the boss
around here.* This open-aired prison. My whimsical companion. Let's
assume we are coterminous. Let's end here.

HOW I PREPARE MYSELF TO BE LOVED BY THE TULIP BREEDER

First I wake up and try not to see him, pretend to be alone. I keep hearing *body aware, body aware* and rub the writing callous on my fingertip. There are over one hundred access points for bathing, laundering, and praying, meridians on the river. Mama. There are other people. Yet still, we will meet at eight o'clock, somewhere French. There are other people. Yet still, I am an internal ocean, seismic activity, a Jesus corpse, a way of holding space. Daily, I discover gradualness, a way of shaping space. Today, if you become frightened….

Daily, unshowered, we brunch at three. Then I press my fingertips to the ground, knees, chin, chest, and with each repetition become thankful that there are no answers. Press the tops of my feet into the earth and look for more questions. I consider counting every second for the rest of the day and then change my mind. I finished the dictionary yesterday and will read the last page at noon again today. I hope to be possessed by five. I still find cholera sexy. I touch my skull five times with a stick and allow my soul to leave my body. Some days I believe the world is flat, wish the day was full of only useless things, remember I am only a number, that flowers fall out of fashion. Practice that overlapping stitch, and lower my eyes to recall how you must have felt, blink when I come too close to the answers. Modify a noun. Remember, there are other people. Create a vacancy. Find another start. Begin again.

GOODNIGHT,

To begin there are ways of holding space. Basins of sleep. Full of spies.
Counting backwards, from twenty to one. Only making it to nine.
Nine could be the place of nightmares. Basins of truncated phrases,
each taking their place on my daily "to do" list. There are column
writers and yoga teachers, UPS drivers and cable men, bartenders and
poets. Basins of relationships leading to others. Seven degrees of
separation. Figure this one out.

There is a way to dissolve the unnecessary with counted breath, a way
to see clearly the line from one point to the next, from waking state to
sleep. Dream to waking and the confusion that comes with trying to
figure which is which. Let's try. Let's start counting. Tracking.

There is a constellation in the sky specifically formed to distract me,
my eye, from all of the French words for scarf. There is me, a body
responding to sunrise in repetitive movements. There is pleasure in
this.

What happened to our ideas? Let me show you my enthusiasm.
Counting. There are parts of an engine while running, folded paper
to make origami, the geological layers to press my hands against, the
diagram of a heart, a broken ribcage, tattooed body, ex-lover's anatomy,
future home, fire escape route, my sentences, yours. Everything
inhibiting, but not fatal. Enough is enough.

Dear and Sincerely,
All the best.

ACKOWLEDGMENTS

Grateful acknowledgment goes to the editors of the following publications, in which versions of these poems first appeared (some in different forms): *Parthenon West Review, Hotel Amerika, EOAGH,* and *La Fovea.*

In "Seven More Wonders, and then some" the phrase "invisible architecture" is borrowed from Barbara Guest.

In "Let Me Show You My Snow Globe Collection" the line "we are a landscape of all we have seen" is quoted from Isamu Noguchi, "You are the one who writes and is written" is a line from Edmond Jabès.

Some of these poems appeared in the chapbook, "An Aorta with Branches, A Travelogue," published by sunnyoutside press. Thank you, David McNamara.

So much gratitude goes to Spuyten Duyvil and Heather Woods for believing in these words and giving them a home to breathe. Heartfelt thanks to Truong Tran and Anhvu Buchanan for always being my biggest supporters and not allowing this book to be buried. Toni Mirosevich, thank you for shepherding these poems when they were first birthed. Friends, teachers, editors, thank you.

DEBORAH WOOD lives with her family on the coast of Massachusetts. She has published poetry and fiction in numerous journals. Her chapbook, "An Aorta with Branches, A Travelogue" is available from sunnyoutside press.

www.ingramcontent.com/pod-product-compliance
Lightning Source LLC
Chambersburg PA
CBHW031249120626
46545CB00007B/2727